Manga Drawing For Beginners:

How to Draw Manga Comics Male, Female Characters and Objects, Manga Drawing Art and Sketching, Pencil Drawing Techniques, Lessons and Exercises Guide

By

Angela Pierce

Table of Contents

Manga Drawing For Beginners: How to Draw Manga Comics Male, Female Characters and Objects, Manga Drawing Art and Sketching, Pencil Drawing Techniques, Lessons and Exercises Guide

By Angela Pierce

Introduction

Manga animations could possibly form the greater part of animation heroes and stories given chance. Their sheer imagination and variety of characters is in itself mind-boggling. With so many possibilities, there rarely is a limit to what you can draw and call it a manga character. You could choose to draw a disfigured dragon and call it Aku, the Villain in Samurai Jack, or you could opt to use straight cut lines to draw the masculine face of Grim Jaw of Bleach. Whatever approach you take, you will always have some room to flex your muscle and skill.

Even though manga drawing might be this lenient, you still have to dedicate yourself to learning the basics before you can fully graduate as a manga artist. The following guide will take you through the basic introduction phases of the job and also teach you how to draw the most essential parts of a manga character. After this, you will have what it takes to take on the manga world and take a shot at even the most complex characters out there.

Chapter 1. Basic Manga Drawing Techniques

Manga are drawings that are basically based on traditional Japanese drawing techniques. Manga is one of the most popular comics for their versatility to depict meaning in wide range of genres. Manga drawings may look complicated but when you master basic drawing techniques, it becomes easier to draw different characters. The biggest problem you will encounter when drawing any manga character is the proportionality of the image. Either the heads looks relatively big or small compared to the body. We will come at that point but let's see the tools required to draw a manga.

Basic Requirements

To draw manga you will require to have basic drawing tools. This will include: a pencil for drawing; an 8.5"x11" Paper, this is the ideal size of drawing space you may require; a standard 12" Ruler for measurements; a Work Space to draw your stuff; an Eraser to undo your mistakes; and coloring pencils or crayons. These are some of basic tools, although you

may require additional ones for an enhanced display. Due to advancement in technology, you may only require a software for drawing.

Proportionality

One of the important things to note when drawing a proportionate character is to count the number of "heads tall". It is imperative to know that a human body proportions fit within a fairly standard range. In modern drawing, the head is commonly used as the basic unit of measurement. In this regard, the head is defined as the distance from the top of the head to the chin. Therefore, an average human is considered to be 7-and-a-half heads tall when you include the body and the head.

Other times you may want to use the character's size to depict the drawing as either superior or inferior compared to a typical human.

For superiority, a figure which is 8 heads tall depicts nobility or grace, while 8 ½ will depict a heroic figure or a demi-god. The superiority is mainly complemented by the ability to draw a wider chest and longer legs due to additional length.

Basic Parts

The head: this is the first part you should which also acts as the reference point to the rest of the body.

Hair: Take some time to define what kind of hair the manga should have as this is one of the main features that will determine the character.

Eyes: Like the hair, the eyes are the first impression the manga creates to the audience. Note that males and females have a differences in the shape of their eye.

Facial expressions: This is complemented by the size of the face, eyes, and the mouth.

Limbs: note the shoulder are relatively the equal length as the elbow to the wrist. Adult should have longer limbs as compared to children.

Culture and Tastes

It's important to understand the setting of your manga character. The setting may include the location, and historical timing the action is taking place. In addition, you may want to consider the cultural context of the manga character. This will mainly be important when you want to trigger deep emotional response from the audience. The cultural aspect will determine the physical appearance of the manga that in turn reflects the beliefs, opinions of a certain people, which brings about emotional connection. For instance, in many western cultures a body that has 5% longer legs than a normal individual is considered to be more attractive.

Even though manga characters are not completely human, you have to pay attention that most tend to model on the perfect human body. Tall slender legs, beautiful eyes, chiseled abs and busty characters are preferable. Learning how to exaggerate these aspects of your manga drawing without making it look ridiculous could help you attain a perfect character. For a start, try modeling your drawing on something that exists. Once you have mastered this, you can go ahead and try altering proportions of different body parts to come up with your own unique character.

Chapter 2. Drawing Basic Manga Characters

Manga characters are some of the most popular comics. They started in Japan during the 19th century and continue to marvel with their ability to depict different characters and emotions across various story telling genres. When drawing a manga, one of the main impressions is how the manga resembles the typical human, animal or object. This mainly includes: gender, age, and the size of the manga character. To understand how to draw a manga with certain body traits, we will look at major differences between the main sexes: male and female.

Male/Female

It is important to note that, to get the best looking manga you will need to know how to correctly manipulate the body's proportions. To get this right, you will first need to get the correct proportions of the head as this forms the basis for the rest of the body. Although most people find it harder to draw males compared to females, drawing a male does not take long either.

Naturally, the male will have a different look compared to a female, the main difference being average males appearing bigger than females. Therefore, whenever you have both male and female characters in your drawing realize the need for the male to appear taller.

Start with a stick-man sketch on the page. Draw the head and include the hairline and the beard. Males as also known not to accentuate with their eyelashes, and the manga should either have little or no eyelashes. The hair need to be standing up or messy to depict the masculinity.

The male will need to look more muscular as opposed to smooth like, curvy outline seen in women. When drawing the manga male, the shoulders should look expanding and larger than the hipline, even when depicting a timid male by using narrow shoulders, the hips should still be lesser. The torso should not curve in much, either is should be seen to expand out. The hips should be narrower, with no constriction at the waist. The male legs need to show muscle in heroic characters, or just skinnier for an average manga.

To depict a strong male face, the manga needs to have a wider cheekbone and jawline. Handsome men are depicted as darker in their skin texture and dominant males are seen to have box-like face.

Clothes should be based more on the culture and taste of the audience. Often males wear baggy jeans and t-shirts with little or no accessories. Female

Start with the head by drawing a circle then put angled shape at the bottom of the circle for the chin and jawline. A female's face should not be very wide and should be thinner compared to a male.

When drawing the eyes, make the eyelashes longer as women's beauty is accentuated a bit by their eyelashes. Also make small curved strokes for the eyebrows as females tend to have less of them. The neck should be long and slender. Note that a thick neck may make a female look like a young girl.

The secret of drawing is to keep the waist as slender as possible with broad hips. A female will have a curve in at the stomach. Also the pelvis should be bigger compared to male and the hips need to extend a bit on the outside. These two, together with the breasts form the basic contours when drawing the abdomen of a female character. The breasts are drawn from the armpit line and enough space is also created between the breasts.

The breasts and the nipples should appear to face outward. To adjust the size of the breast, raise or lower the underside of the breast - larger breasts have a lower and heavy underline. A female with wide shoulders looks more feminine mostly when the hips are also seen to stick out. When drawing nude or semi-nude females, the navel should be a little bit below the waist and a bit above the crotch, the crotch itself can either be flat or mounded. There should be an opening between the thighs and the crotch, while the buttock should appear firm.

To depict fertility/attractiveness in a woman's face, the Manga should appear with a wider face, the lips should be fuller, and eyebrows should be higher. Beautiful females are drawn with a fairer skin, this may need more coloring of the skin. In western cultures, an ideal beautiful woman should also have blonde hair - you can use curved strokes to make the hair look blonde.

Choose the clothing depending on the location the action is taking place. Other factors that will determine the females wear is the time of day, and the message you as the drawer wants to pass across. You can create a wide variety of female figures just by changing the type of clothes.

Children

Start with the head by drawing a circle. In children's drawing the head should be round and appear to be larger compared to other parts of the body. The height of a child less than 12 years should be 5 heads tall or less, while a teenage height should range between 5 to 7 heads.

Since the body of a child is yet to fully develop, avoid making well-structured body lines and try to make it seem a bit round.

The eyes should be big and round and the distance between the eyes and the nose should be short. Avoid overemphasizing on the nose. The jawline should be less distinct in younger children. You have to make the neck shorter and thicker unlike in adults where it appears long and slender. Make the character hips and chest to be flat.

The fingers are one of the major characteristics that define who is a child and an adult. When drawing a child, the shorter the fingers, the younger the child looks. The wrists and ankles should be relatively thick. The hands and the legs should be appear not fully extended even when drawing a big kid.

Basically, when drawing a child, follow the same techniques like you are drawing an adult but make the legs, torso and arms shorter.

Objects

You can draw various objects using the manga styles. If you are a beginner, mastering how to draw manga objects can help you understand some important basics of drawing a human. You can first start by drawing simple things like lines, circles, rectangles and others. This may first seem boring, but in the end it will be of great benefit.

Draw perspective objects, these are objects that reduce in size as they get further off the distance. This means the nearer the object, the bigger it looks. To get the right perspective, you will need to portray the object in the correct and realistic way. Knowing how to draw basic perspective objects will usher you to more complicated objects which have three dimensions like cubes and cylinders.

Learning how to shade objects makes your image appear more appealing. 2D objects can take 3D shapes if they are shaded in a certain way. To master this, you would need to understand how light if reflected when it falls on an object. Correct shading can also indicate the time of the day, the environment, and even the weather conditions. This plays a key role in complementing other characters in a drawing.

Also, you can use the object to learn how to apply colors. This will help you create beautiful and interesting Manga characters.

Chapter 3. Getting Different Body Parts Right

There are different ways to draw the manga body depending on whether it is a female or male drawing. It is important to consider the proportions of the figure whenever you will add details. For a more dynamic character, you may have to go through different tutorials get it right. The important thing is to ensure that you know what each part needs to look like to achieve a perfect cartoon like figure. How different parts are drawn will influence the anime's character.

Hairstyles

This is the trickiest part to get right. This is because there are different styles each with its own unique technique. The most interesting part about drawing manga hair is the fact that it can be complex or simple at the same time. You need to learn how to draw simple hair using basic techniques.

The first thing is to draw the head of your manga character. A basic frame is important as it provides a road map on which to work on. The manga heads will depend on the gender females having a rounder head while males will have faces that are more angular. The next thing is to look at the hair type. You should consider making it a little crazy as seen in some of the most famous characters that have had absurd hairs, which in a way influences their character. Consider the place where the parting goes, whether you want bangs or fringes and if the hairstyle you choose matches the character's personality.

Mark the hair outline on the character's head. The side of the head should be an equal distance from the top of the head to the top of the hairstyle. Draw the basic outline of the hair paying attention to the guided marks you made earlier. Detail and shape the hair, color and shade the hair and complete the facial character.

Hands

A good number of manga styles are based on natural drawing meaning you can start by drawing realistically. When drawing make sure, you factor in the different spheres, cylinders and the wedge shape attached to a box to make the hand. Start by sketching the box, which will to stand for the palm of the hand. On it, sketch four circles to take care of the fingers. The wedge shape will accommodate the thumb. You then have to sketch the fingers. Using a similar technique you should draw the opposite side of the hand using you own hand as reference.

There is a second method to draw the hand of a manga character. You start by drawing a circle or ball using a pencil and five sticks needed in order the ball to get attached for them to serve as fingers. And if you want something to remind you should have put markers where the fingers of its joints are. Make shapes that are in cylindrical in form over the sticks in order to shape the hand. You can then draw the forearm and creases on the ball. Using a marker and eraser, darken silhouette and erase unnecessary lines from your earlier drawing. The second drawing technique is more impressive.

Feet

To draw a proper manga foot you need to learn that the foot consist of basic forms. These forms are divided into three namely the cylinder for the shin, half peanut for the front and roundish shape for the heel. The foot is an important element of a manga character because it represents action when the figure is illustrated. Foot angles, positions and movements are part of the most important factors to consider when drawing figures and visible body actions that can communicate specific messages. Drawing feet can be intimidating but as manga artists, you cannot avoid it. With a systematic guide it is possible to get the foot shape right.

In a basic and simplified structure, you are not required to paint the entire leg but rather boots and shoes. It is important to get an important depiction, proportion and expression without overdoing it. This is more important than putting a bunch of wrinkles and bumps. Getting the foot shape and proportion right should be your main concern first. Make sure you minimize the lines and add details later on with thinner line details. By the end of the drawing, you will have a fine pictorial representation that you can paint to depict shoes or boots depending on how you want the manga character to appear.

Bodies

This will depend on the gender of anime you want to draw. For the female, the first thing to draw is a stick figure, the head's circle, tiny circles for the joint location and small triangles for the hands and feet. You can connect these shapes using lines to make a general body framework. You can then draw the head and torso and add feminine details such as breasts and slender waistlines in addition to making the hips slightly wide. Draw the limbs, sketch a few more details on hair and clothing, and finish up with coloring the drawing.

The male body has a slight variation where you draw a stick, a circle for the head, small circles for the joints and small triangles for the hands and feet just as in the female body. The head and torso are drawn next making sure that the man's trunk is broader compared to the female's slender waistline. You should hen draw the limbs making them look bulkier because of the muscles. Sketch more details on hair and clothing and finally color it appropriately. Check out the different body drawing techniques before settling for the one you are most comfortable with.

Faces

Adjusting the front view of a manga face is always easy. However, this is boring and it is what everyone does when starting out. You should picture the head like a ball and a line crossing where the eyes should be.

Rotate the ball around and use the lines to give your character dynamics head angles.it is not necessary to follow a rigid formula to confine yourself to the guidelines. The important thing is to convey motion and use the lines to guide you.

You need to create a profile view, which is not always easy to get. Depending on the age of the character, facial appearance should be adjusted to fit their age. For the children making the eyes bigger and lower to the chin will do the trick while teenagers or young adults the face needs to be narrower for females and flat chinned for males. You should thicken the neck as well. For the older generation the shape of the face does not change such apart from a few wrinkles, which you need include around the mouth, eyes and forehead.

Other body parts

The only way to notice a difference in your drawings is to ensure that you are approaching it with a skilled artist's perspective. As you draw and continue to realize that your drawing is your thing then you should consider doing it professionally. You need to get some training on the basic drawing of manga shapes and figures.

The first thing is to ensure that you plan for the drawing and not rush to draw. Planning the figure gives you a rough concept of that the general figure should be like. Never sketch something ad finalize it without looking at the basic concept and overlooking it as a whole. It is important to plan a pose in skeletal lines or guidelines to finalize the functional body parts.

A weak foundation only mean weak finalization, which is the last thing you want for your anime picture. Train on how to sketch quickly especially when you have a vision of what you want to draw. Skeletal lines are crucial to draw out before drawing the literal structures such as the limbs and body structure. You should take some time to sketch different poses with certain references in mind. You will be able to produce dynamic poses by hand if you practice more.

Chapter 4. Perspectives in Manga Drawing

To be a great anime or manage drawer you must be able to use methods that are easy to get impressive results. You should change the construction guidelines severally to get it right. There are different styles and perspectives that different artist use to achieve results.

Comparing how different spaces of guidelines affects the resulting image regardless of the body part being drawn. For example, when drawing the face you should consider the construction guidelines that affect the resulting manga lines. The spacing of the lines in relation to each other will always place each part of the face to its respective guidelines.

With the right perspective, you can always come up with something that will work regardless of how puffed up different body parts are. For instance, with the right perspective, you could easily draw Naruto and make him look like Jonny Bravo. Alternatively, you could puff him up a bit and make him look really monstrous and towering over the building. Perspective, in this case, is all about playing with an object and its environment to elicit new feels and perceptions.

Understand how to draw anime faces with systematic drawing lesson

Profiles are helpful when drawing faces and heads in any style. This is because they help artists understand the differences in people's heads. This helps familiarize with the face of the character when drawing. Shapes can vary but regardless of it the side view is what affects what can be seen from the front view. If you want to know the face better, look at his or her profile.

Illustrations for drawing human faces in anime profile view

Start with a simple circle structure. A circle shape is the perfect shape for an anime or manga face or head. Draw horizontal line through the center of the circle making the circle separate in tow halves. Cut one-half of the circle also horizontally at the bottom part of the circle. Draw a line down the center vertically and a diagonal line from the left side of the center horizontal line. With these guidelines in place and an anime profile ready, you can draw the features clearly.

There are many things to consider when drawing a manga pictorial representation. There is no technique that stands out as the best. Different artist have used varied styles to achieve unique and outstanding manga features. It is important to stick to the basics of drawing and you will be fine. Make sure you remain within the guidelines of drawing an anime without losing your individuality and personal touch on style.

Reading different tutorials on manga drawing can enrich your knowledge and style and make you a better artist. It is not illegal to expound your perspectives by looking at how other artist views things. After all, it is a creative world out there.

Conclusion

Even though learning how to draw in theory could boost your skill and confidence, it is up to you to try out the things you learn in person. Try implementing the drawing techniques when drawing your favorite manga characters. If you do not have any favorite characters or something to model on, it is advised that you latch onto something. Drawing with a visual impression on your mind increases your efficiency and imaginations more. You will most probably come up with better drawings or have something to compare your handiwork against and gauge your progress in the art.

I want to personally thank you for reading my book. I hope you found information in this book useful and I would be very grateful if you could leave your honest review about this book. I certainly want to thank you in advance for doing this.

If you have the time, you can check my other books too.